10

I Want Your Chair

I Want
Your Chair

Poems by
Elaine Schwager

Rattapallax Press

Rattapallax Press

532 La Guardia Place, Suite 353, New York, NY 10012
212-560-7459
e-mail: rattapallax@hotmail.com
website: www.rattapallax.com

Ram Devineni, *Publisher*

Printed in the United States of America.

ISBN: 1-892494-08-6 (paperback)
ISBN: 1-892494-18-3 (clothbound)
LCCN: 99-069799

Dedication

This book is dedicated to

my grandparents:
Leopold Schwager
Sabena Teller Schwager
Julius Weihl
Bettina Hammel Weihl

my father
Carl Schwager
who believed the human voice was the
most beautiful instrument of all

and

my mother
Inge Weihl Schwager
who said
"life goes in cycles and no one is spared."

Acknowledgments

I wish to acknowledge the editors of the following publications in which some of the poems in this book first appeared: *Writ, Literal Latté, Rattapallax, Jüdische Gemeindezeitung, Minding the Gap,* and *Drunken Boat.*

I am grateful to my first mentors Paul Blackburn and Louis Simpson for their steady, warm encouragement in my early writing life; Roger Greenwald, for a lifetime of being a reader of my poems, his careful review of the manuscript and helpful suggestions; Charles Fishman, Bill Kushner and Stanley Marcus for their helpful comments and editing at crucial points in my reviewing and restructuring the manuscript; Deedee Agee, Nina Bogin-Farber, Linda Feigleson, Mickey Friedman, Barbara Goldberg, Elizabeth Hurvich, Philip Schultz, Joanna Scott, and Marilyn Steiner who have encouraged and supported my writing; Lavonna Gabriel for her many forms of sustenance.

In addition, I wish to thank Mark Gotbaum for the artwork on the cover and Glenn Davis for the section line drawings.

Special thanks and love to my children Carl and Julia for changing the course of history and their ongoing inspiration, and my husband Marvin for his generosity and support.

Finally, I want to thank Ram Devineni, publisher of Rattapallax Press, for designing and printing this book. I am grateful for his belief in this work and his courage.

CONTENTS

I. Was That God Asking Us To Listen?

II. Lost Violin

III. The Rose Light

IV. I Want Your Chair

V. Free

We've inherited hope
the gift of forgetting.
You'll see how we give
birth among the ruins.

Wisława Szymborska
from "Notes from a Nonexistent Himalayan Expedition."
Translated by Stanislaw Barańczak and Clare Cavanagh.

I

Was That God Asking
Us To Listen?

The Archives

The Librarian asked if I knew the City.
I said "Frankfurt." Then she disappeared,
came back with a black
atlas-sized book.

Among the pages, my grandmother's
printed name so matched
what she was called,
and called herself, her life

condensed there. Generations
met where my eyes touched
the letters. "You know
I am looking for you,"

I thought, at the end
of your half-life,
still radiating
a dying that will never be done.

Verschollen it says
of your date of death.
Unbekannt of the place.
You are the beginning

of thought that cries
below words, where clarity is
a tiny lens and reason
weak as a limp in a race

with wings. I lose a breath
as an ocean loses a wave.
What is in that space
that is neither memory nor event

yet happened
and is never forgotten?
What is that place
where a grandchild searches

for your lap
on which to rest
the weight of your absence
and leave there

the flowering of no end?

She Lives Here

The gravestones are pieces of pink and
green, pieces piled in clusters,
clusters lined in rows. My grandmother
has no headstone nor piece

of a headstone. She has no representation
in the cemetery or anywhere
in the world. Perhaps she ended up ash,
smoke, a stack of bones, or a body

along the roadside trying to run away
from the black charcoal she already knew
no one would recognize
as her and the sorrow

she did not want
to be
the rest of her life. We find
her name on a wall

on a 1 x 2 inch plaque. We put stones
on the narrow ledge above
BETTINA

Seventeen

When she got out of the cattle car,
the poor Polish workers whispered,
"Say you are seventeen." She did
and the SS men in stiff gray,
glossed shoes, buttons and hair took her

aside and taught her how
to direct her people to the right
and left. "Let the children stay
with the old people." They said,
"we will take good care of them."

Her pregnant sister with two small children,
her mother, younger sisters,
father, younger brother,
grandmother and grandfather went right
in the direction called "good care."

She was alone when the faceless
dry voice asked again,
"How old are you?"
"Seventeen," she heard
herself say and was pointed

left, to live
ceaselessly
asking herself how a lie
could be both
mask and prayer.

In the Same Sky

Every night I see my sister ready to give
birth, turning to the same
God who saved me. Her two thin boys, like
timeless cries

of innocence are draped around her.
Why was she chosen
to watch her children burn
to feel life that should have

just begun, die inside her?
Why was she chosen to question why
I was chosen
to praise the silence

that would not answer her?
I have been obedient
and kept my heart a grave
for bodies to be buried in

and for the questions left in her
unanswered. But still
I cannot sleep
in the same night

she dies in.

The Tunnel

The even row of lights in the tunnel,
like Kaddish candles' white flames, flicker

in memory. I wish the mind had no permit
for such storage and burial, to distort

and then retrieve what was lost. The water presses
its tons of iciness against the concrete

walls. I picture it breaking through
as your life broke through mine

Mother. All those years, all those bodies
congealed in the glacial sheets you wrapped around me

each night. It was your right
to forget and my duty to remember

how your mother sent you away, knowing she would die
that she would never see you again. I saw

your blue child's eyes in the window
of a train, your black curls just combed,

your dress pressed and chosen
to attract attention.

In your small hands, a book your mother
read to you over and over, a ragged stuffed possum

you lay with each night, feigning death,
sensing there were many to whom your breathing

was a crime, and photos you stole
that your mother stole back from you

and then reluctantly gave you. One
was of your father standing in uniform

against a gun-metal sky,
another of your mother's face

forever adoring, incapable of dying in the silver air
she inhabited on the paper scrolled tight

in your hand. She taught you how to find the love
she'd never be able to give you. Every time you lost

someone, you went back to find
her. You ask me to come along,

to be there when you discover I am
the one you want. I am the one

crying for you at the station,
the one leaving you as the train pulls away.

Why did you think I was so clean
and empty? A perfect baby girl born in America

to shape into anything you pleased? I wanted
to find love elsewhere,

but I couldn't leave you
to pursue pleasures

so much smaller
than the lives that were wasted.

Both of us tried to find our way out
of the same nightmare. But we weren't

dreaming, we were tunneling
through the ice.

What Will You Picture in the Haze?

There you are
in your hospital gown—
no glasses, hearing aid
makeup or jewels, stripped

to the hunched child you were
in the shadow between lives
in a booming city
and a bombed-out ghetto—

a warm face pressed against mother
as Nazis came to char your fables.
Your soft eyes are already smoke
in their minds. Here you are

waiting to be numbed and cut
so the lens of your eye can be replaced,
your vision returned.
Around us are ordinary people

in surgical gowns. You see yourself
in their clean smiles
as someone too temporary
for them to know. They bring a wheelchair

and let me follow toward surgery.
At the double door they say,
"Take a left and a left
and the second elevator

down to the second floor. We'll call for you
in the waiting room. "I could not tell
if the skies were darkening
or if the sun was gone.

Someone came in with a burger, chips and soda
in a cardboard box. By then you were under.
There's a history in that darkness. Maybe
I'm there, listening to you tell me

the loss of vision is nothing
compared to the loss of a mother
or father, a home, love
that should have carried you

through this continual drifting
in anesthetized space. I think you are
seeing your mother
sending you away

with no ticket back,
no last embrace that won't let you go.
Will it matter if one
lens replaces another?

What comes alive in sleep
you see more vividly than
anything you see
with open eyes.

Quiet

"Nothing to be
concerned about, "the doctor said, but
as he pressed near this new hardness,
it hurt." Just a few years left to be

myself, "she thought and bought a new TV
with remote and digital clarity to sit
surrounded by, so she could be the eye
of its storm, trying not to wish

the rain would stop as it falls relentless
as listening. She started to dust,
as she had when the hospital called
to say her husband was dead.

She likes the deep dark
grainy wood spotless and shining.
On the reflecting surface she sees
herself sing in perfect pitch

"Bluebird, bluebird through my window,
Oh Johnny, I am tired."
She is a baby, fragile as a sparrow
in the middle of a field of snow:

each direction exactly as cold
as the others. The song is all
that's not over—and the fear
that it is. She wants—

though the parts of her life don't
add up—once to not approximate
but to be the equation
solved, to be more than

the dust she is made of, idling
on surfaces she can't see beyond.

Forgetting to Live

You can get fascinated with the machinery,
the way the switch is released
that lowers the coffin into the earth
on green straps. The rabbi stands
at the foot of the grave,
the line of his black silk cloak
skewing the flurries of snow.

He reads from his black book:
"He will rest in the embrace
of eternity." The snow
melts on the unfamiliar
Hebrew letters. "It is in
the thoughts that will continue
to enrich our lives
that he will find immortality."

Your last words wished for others
to go further than the train of cattle cars
circling the town on the rim
of the pitch-black night, further than the town
waiting for the train, further than the night
sitting pitch-black, too frightened to move.

You held no grudge, all forgiven, but
your pain was hurting me, the pain
had spread—cancer
metastasized—though corners of you
yearned for life.

You touched me with songs
breathed into my hair—a softness

too gentle to understand. Lullabies blew
into my dark room. Warm nights clung
to the notes that grew
like seeds and with them
I sprang up in the meadow
of your un-lived life.

I don't know why
you kept forgetting to live. You dreamt
the hospital left you
in the cold and you were tied down
in a train and the train
was taking you away.

Each on our side of your bed, your brother and I
talked across your body, afraid
you heard enough to feel regret.
He wanted me to know you wanted
no part of the bourgeoisie, you went
against their wishes—and sang.

The survivors clutch themselves:
woolen figures angled in the snow.
Breath gracelessly clouds
the light above the grave. Your life is
the daydream that won't be
extinguished in this murmuring, damp
gray. I refuse to go
under with you. I refuse to mourn.

Civil Disobedience 1938

Hannah put her only diamond into a blue cloth button, sewed it into a worn blue dress, and sent it fourth class mail to an aunt in America.

Her aunt lifted the unwearable garment from the undesirable paper. The card fell. It read "Happy Birthday from the 3 of us." The 3 had points like barbed wire sticking out and was darkened and smudged.

It was not her aunt's birthday and there were four of them. The dress was the wrong size and there was no return address. Her aunt thought of giving the dress to The Salvation Army or her cleaning girl's daughter, but decided to hang it in her closet until she understood the darkened, barbed 3.

Each morning she looked at the dress, wishing it could speak louder than the news blaring as she dusted and straightened her world. The news spoke only of local thefts and traffic delays, the weather and who was running for this office and that.

One morning the dress fell off its hanger. From the weight of what? As she lifted it up, the third button bulged bigger than the rest. She bit it open and wondered why the news didn't report: the world is in danger of a life being worth only this.

Unopened

Lines around his eyes
laugh without him.
They are remains
of pleasure he took
in everything before

he saw getting older as
getting worse and chances
as deep lines in a carving
that defined a picture
he didn't want to see.

Tears, like breathing,
move in and out of him
like the knife they sliced
his mother open with
when he was four,

as if she was only meat,
only that which a knife could kill.
In his blood is the knife's point,
telling him, in its
permanent existence,

"This is who you are
all your struggles with yourself
will not reveal a man of
peace." His last pulse turns into
a moment—a seed that will be

his whole story.

The Place Left by a Body

"Who dies at a yes or no."
— Primo Levi

Like a dog I scratch the dirt,
trying to get out of the darkness
their stories, stories still
wandering free of words
and the meaning of words.

I dig to find why each story ended
at the moment it did, to get out
of the darkness what is
deeper than death. It is
my turn to take everything

valuable from their lives. The diamonds,
houses, gold fillings, thick black
hair, leather shoes have been found
and named. I hit on a minacious silence
in which the rotting ash smells of babies

burning. I am a face
turned away from my child
to be kissed
by darkness. I feel no envy
for the living

who are afraid to die,
afraid to save
the dying, afraid to shoot
and not to shoot
afraid.

Day Trip

In Worms, the synagogue
burnt to the ground
was recreated. The *mikvah*
was as it was then, cold stone
where obedient women
had bathed to protect men
from their blood.

Now a community stripped
of its Jews, Worms has a museum
where a dollhouse family sits perfectly
dressed at a well-set table,
in a tastefully furnished room,
breaking plaster matzoh and waiting

for Elijah. There is a graveyard:
under rocks, shredding notes
written to dead prophets,
begging the past to return
wisdom to the present. There the living
held a minyan. Ten men

put handkerchiefs on their heads.
Each stared at a different tombstone
in a mudhole splashed with sun. Shards
of glassy memory tore open
their garments
to a wilderness of sky.

Landscape on the Way to Buchenwald

Cows in dense pink light
cows by painted silver water
cows in the Goethe museum
in Frankfurt are missing
in the leafy green landscape,
the cool waterfalls
are without them. They
are gathered in the thick
paint of summer heat
where they would not choose
to go.

Was That God Asking Us To Listen?

God was the whole
bloody mess—the ovens and the gas
and the children dressed in white slippers
and soft shirts before they were given as fuel
for fire. God was the dumb silence

behind it all
in which there was shuddering and prayer.
How could we expect God to listen,
when he was filling the graves, blocking off air,
using the dead to scream

as loud as he could, it seemed, for no good
reason, but to turn the tables
on us. He made us hear the prisoners
of fire living their death,
without which God could not continue

to obliterate laughter. God was the tears
and the offering and the not
listening, and the days of no bread and then bread
again, the yell of pain that will be our lives
forever.

Arrival

We got word,
via cousins
that our grandparents
never made it
to a concentration
camp.
Even though
they had paid for
their own
one way
train ticket,
they were
slaughtered
brutally
before
they arrived.

"Details
too gruesome
to send
without
request.
Do you
want them?"
they ask
in English
so we
understand.

"Please," I beg, "Send
everything. Let
the reason
I've been
crying and
unable to cry
my whole life arrive."

The Internet

As an untimely snow falls
on a cow licking its salt
cube, a thick-billed, brown-headed
cowbird nudges a sparrow's eggs out of its nest and
drops its own eggs in. The sparrow babies will die
as spring creeps around the globe
from the East.

A photo from 1905 is on a website.
My slaughtered great grandparents,
grandfather, great aunts, great uncles are posed
in the positions, outfits and expressions we see now.
Their bright yellow hearts, like yolks,
were expunged and splintered
light through time.

The picture is downloaded, passed on
by clicking "Address Book" twenty times,
forwarded to the children of the children
of the murdered. The portrait is stared at like memory
on the electronic screen, as if the internet
existed all along as one collective
unconscious we are now realizing.

Photograph of White Asparagus on a Green Plate

Two Germans, two Jews,
two descendants
of Nazis, two descendants
of Jews killed by Nazis

talk in Frankfurt over beer and white
asparagus on a green plate, posing, as if for
a photograph. We are not hungry or afraid of
each other. *We pay with silver and gold*

credit cards. We are not one of the millions
killed or one of the ones who killed millions.
We sit like bishops and rabbis contemplating
how evil can flourish in hope and hope arise

out of evil. We exchange
phone numbers and addresses and plan
meetings to discuss what it felt like to be
naked before those who judged

if you were to be killed, raped or enslaved and
what it felt like to be the one who judged.
We are the children and grandchildren of someone
killed, raped or allowed to work till they were frozen-

white asparagus stretched
out on the grass. We are the children and grandchildren
of those who killed, raped or forced another to work—
armies in the white wilderness—

rows of tall asparagus, spreading like thickets.
Strings of asparagus hang
from our teeth. We see across the table
eyes of the dead, eyes of murder.

We look at each other
with a form of love
that cannot see backwards
or forward.

II

Lost Violin

First Child

Emerging from history so softly,
you want to be totally surrounded
by the parts you love—a nipple
to suck, hair to pull.

You reach to eat a speck
on the floor that shines
as the sun comes in thin lines
through the blinds.

Pinks and yellows rise, helium balloons
over the Hudson. Cars honk, shovels
scrape the sidewalk. You smile at each
sound and try to touch the shifting light.

There's one kind of crying that nothing will stop
except holding you at the window
to see the lit red Sloan's sign
across the street

or taking you out to listen to horns
and sirens. City baby,
lullabied by clatter
hushed by traffic and neon signs,

you feed me melted cookies
with your chocolate hands
the same way I feed you. My mistakes
come back to me

in those chubby fists.

31

Picking Pumpkins

The rain stops; shadows appear like holes
in the burnt red grass. We get on the hay wagon

headed for the pumpkin fields. A scent of green
is the absence of green. In your Old Navy

sweats and muddy sneakers the four of you drop
like dark ink into my listening.

When the wagon stops
Michi jumps off and becomes

one of the colors of the field. Leah
leaves her print in the steady air

spots Christina and runs
to help her roll a pumpkin up the hill.

Julia's iridescent parka flickers
in a breeze, her limbs full

of play in this brilliant orange
and yellow world. We load the blue

wagon. I pull uphill, feeling
the tug back down. The not-yet-dusted,

soon-to-be jack-o'-lanterns lodge
in their muddy world. We all imagine

the crescent dark moon cut to smile
in an orange face around which will grow

party magic—crowds and candles fluttering
in a mist of music. In the smell of fire

hills sit close
to that electric violet

you find at the center
of a stove light. And the black

around the edges begins
to end all imagery.

Parsley

Carl enters my office with three plastic bags
of greens. "Which one is parsley?" he asks,
dropping them all in my lap.

"These two," I say.

"Two?" he asks. "Why two?"

"One is good parsley and one is bad parsley."

"How do I know which is which?"

"Try them both. One will make you deadly ill
and one will nourish you."

"So why try them both?" he asks.

"How else will you know?"

"Can't you try one?" he asks, "and then tell me?"

"You won't believe me.
And the one that could kill me might heal you."

"What if I pick the bad one first and I die?"

"You will know before you are dead
and the good parsley will be in your hands
to nullify its effects."

"Are you sure?" he asks.

"No! Both may be good parsley, or both bad."

"But that would be worse," he says.
"If they are both bad, there would be no good
to bring me back to life."

"Then have no parsley," I say. "Cook nothing
that requires it. Use only plain salt and pepper."

"But that would be sad," he wants to say. "These greens
seem to be life itself."

Yes, the green of the world
giving scent to the rain, moist lawns
in blackening cemeteries, the ferns indistinguishable
from shadows in the woods. They have a fixed
destiny, unlike yours.

Riding

"It is because he can betray you
that riding is wonderful,"
Julia said: it was why she loved being taken
by a horse up an ice-drizzled mountain.

"I had my escape planned,
how I'd throw my foot over the side
if the horse fell and tumble off
just a split second before

his death." All that time, my mind was on
white hairline paths—stubbornly curled
ice lying firm in the winter sun
up and down the slopes. The calm coppers

and smoky yellows splashed as if
by trembling hands along grim ghettos
of green, and tiny sparks
of lavender straying from unmapped streams.

"You can't control
the horse," Julia stated, smiling.
"He has a personality, a mind
of his own. Sometimes I thought so loud,

I know he heard me.
Once when we galloped
and it felt like it wasn't enough to hold on
tight, I prayed for wings."

She was close to a fear
she'd been longing for.
I made hope possible
only by offering no protection.

Though I was right
there, one horse behind
her small straight back and
the black velvet hat,

if the horse made her leap into her
first fall,
she would only be
mine to watch.

TV Light

My son sits in TV light
eating fajitas. He knows TV
is like the mind,
which constructs its own hue
turns itself off and on
and operates on many channels.
He hugs his TV. It's been programmed
to record and go off on command.
He knows too that time is
something to be played with,
and a rerun and a preview
can appear on the same day,
that what's on in the future
has already appeared in the past
and what he has already seen
will come back in perfect replica.
He knows we humans just pretend
we are creating brand new worlds
that will last forever
so we can feel different, he says
from the bugs we crush
as we embrace
the mechanical.

Gravel

Bag of gravel pebbles: a present
from a nature walk. First children,
they say, are hard, come apart
in your hand; you can't hold them
in one shape. His two sides jar
each other and half of him clashes
against me. He needs to fight,
to kick if I bring him close.
I shake the bag of stones
knotted on top. They sound
harmonic, melodic, as my rhythmic motion
continues. Each hard small piece
part of a continuous sound
I hear as if it were concealed
in my own silence.

Orange Day

Today is orange day
in school. My son told me
he'll be having an orange party
that orange is boring
and all they do at the party is
decorate milk cartons with orange
construction paper, use orange crayons,
learn that red and yellow mixed
make orange, paint
orange shapes, eat orange goodies
and drink orange juice.
The only thing that's fun,
he says, is sticking the straw
in the little juice pouch.

Gerbils

They're born purple in large numbers
and sniff their way
to mamma's teat. "The first litter

almost always dies," the pet-
store owner said, "but they'll keep
trying." Sure enough, two neglected

in the far corner of the tank
lie like little burgundy livers on the ground.
The others wiggle, latching on

to the season that is their life
like thawing buds, the clement air
the only gap between them and

their dead sisters. Most of
the second generation survives.
It takes a while to learn to be parents.

Watch the young mother forgetting
the little blackened secrets
sprawled like dance positions

in the litter. Watch her panic
while she looks at eight new wobbling hearts—
tiny volcanoes—that could splatter

on the edge of all she knows.
Will she eat these babies—
fleshy pink stars?

The father's off on the side
inspecting the ones
that died early, but she

is a mound of fur over thirsty red
mouths. I would never call her brave,
honest, dedicated, resilient or determined

to do her best. One could say
simply her body loves
and shivers.

Admittance

My Children
I gather the touch of
your hundreds of kisses
pressed into my skin.

I am the stillness
in your flowering,
shaped by every turn
you take

following the questions
that search
for you. It is
your secrets

I see, spilled
like mouthfuls of baby teeth
with the space for permanence gaping.
This is the absence I serve.

Can't Get Enough of Wanting to Kill

Evil is born along with a sibling, desire
to become a warrior, to fight off
the perfectly loved.
One can't get enough of
wanting to kill.

"Be careful of the soft spot
on his head, "mamma tells me
as she rests him in the hollow
of my goose-bumped arms. Right away
he slips. I imagine

they convict me—
a tot in stripes behind bars.

———————

His toothless face sticks out
between the blond crib rails.

When he cries, I reach
for his blue fleece shape
as for a cloud in a dream
and move in as close as the bars allow.

He pulls my curls till I scream.
Mamma swoops him up like she used to do
with me and tells him
not to hurt me. I hum

invisible songs in angry air
while she hands him perfectly colored toys

44

and ends his day in summery kisses
leaving him sweet and lit from inside.

———————

When he's older, we share a blue room
with sailboat shapes fleeting
on the linoleum ocean floor;
a yellow wooden table
set for two. We pretend we live

in an enormous house
with people we don't want
to be like, orphans playing
alone in a landscape
of dark crystals,

but he wants real tea biscuits and apple juice.
He doesn't believe in unbreakable games
that go on to elegant conclusions.
When he says, "I don't want
to play anymore,"

I run into the kitchen
and tell mamma he fell
out the window.
She drops her knife
and races to my room.

See how easy it is to make people die,
how a lie becomes the same
as what you could have done?

In the White Van

Julia dreams beyond
my dreams for her, while our white van
merely moves ahead.

"Look!" she cries,
"Fairyland is over there—
where the mist is"

and the navy hills deepen
against the streaks
of salmon and lilac. She is petal soft:

amazed we are here between
who we are and what we see
between ourselves and each other.

She wants us to play
more games that name the world.
In her quest, I live again—

Make-up

"All that color makes you mean!"
My daughter shouts, reaches
with a moist tissue to wipe it off.

"Anyway, why is the color
you put on better
than the one that is you?"

So I let her cleanse me
of my disguise.
When the mask is gone

there is a moment
when I expect to be seen
as sick, old, ugly.

I return to the mirror, reapply
rouge, lipstick, eyeliner,
shadow. I need to be

the person she is afraid of,
blind
to what I make her see.

Sixth Birthday

Glossy balloons shrivel by the second,
and the garden is strewn with pails
and party hats and balls.
Now she is less a part of me

and more, and wants to know
why I look sad
why I've yelled
or forgotten. She wakes dreams I've chosen

not to have and grows a language
like skin to keep her unspoken
story—a quiet gleam
undamaged, whole and wild

as any *No* she dares to slip
into our stockinged and smudged lives.
It is this child who now decides
when kisses are wanted,

who weighs and judges
each action, thought and smile
against some flame-tipped kiss
or sea-fresh tenderness

not yet had.

Lolitas Play Catch

In snug tank tops, bell-bottoms,
hair tied tight and high,
they toss a clear globe from hand
to hand. Sneakered, sandaled,
their valentine feet like humming birds
flutter above exploding blossoms.

Alongside the curves of the leaves
they move as space does.
The green threads of their lives
almost thoughts framed
with a canopy of night, star filled.
Each one of them amply silent, amply dark

offers emptiness instead of attention.
Like searchers of mushrooms and olives
in a large green salad
their minds can't break
the habit of fighting
for scarcity. Each feels

herself a lone dark pit
of sky in a bouquet of foliage. The red
handed down from woman to woman
is their dress,
indistinguishable
from a broken heart's blood

gently imprisoned
in the cracks of dark
holding them

49

in their leaf shape.
A glimpse of their beauty,
left untouched, arouses a calm

that believes they are there.

First Kiss

This is it: your body
belongs to your fantasies now.

In your nightmares, God's valet
removes with alcohol-soaked

cotton balls the thin layers
of mind you so obediently took on.

Now that boy who played Pied Piper,
promises to clear a way for you

through rats as his heart
pounds and his notes settle

inside you. There, you can't tell
your puppy from a sneaker or a string

of jewels from the bar of
a cage. And sky seems so like

the skin of raw fish, you think
you should be swimming.

Sweetheart, beware of
gravity, even if you're not

falling. And don't pitch
your ball right

into forgiveness.
You might hit a ghost.

51

Lost Violin

Julia lost the violin she wanted to play
in a dream. She says I said
It was gone forever, then slipped
in the mud near the water
and *I* wasn't there
to help. I know I was
the river and the mud and the violin
and the playing and the forever
and she wished I would be gone
so she could feel her body
warm and heavy by the stones
in her own music, her own
band of yellow light,
where she remains without turning
when I call, "Climb back up,
be careful, come home."

III

The Rose Light

Possessed

At the far end of your sentences,
your perceptions cracked
and the difference between the brightness

of your eyes and your body's stillness
made you seem possessed—the way
carbonation pings inside

a tin can. We glided across
a dance floor, dipping
into depths that outlasted happiness.

I knew your bones, their weight, one moment
hesitant, then determined, and the whole surface
of your body covered my breath.

I was puzzled:
how little was said, how much
it hurt to part. You were just pleased

to be alive. In the fall, we walked
by the piers and listened to boats
rocking against the wooden pilings. Gulls

swept the shore for castaway crumbs, the wind
swirled into dust. You said you were
in transit, on your way to another temporary

post. Strange how that walk by the river
still comes clear as I speak of it, how precisely
words fill in what I didn't understand

then. Memory leaves phrases
that have nothing to do with our lives
as we lived it. Just because we go on,

new events revise the old, and now
another man leans over the railing
by the river talking to me

quietly about the sky.

Monkeying Across Bars of Philosophy

It is the loveliest time of
day and we are trying to kill
this fly.

The dry red flowers of the geranium
press against the glass;
still the sun can't reach them.

You are afraid to start
your life over
in the middle of it.

Why do you want to simplify?
Complications offer
more possibilities.

My hands are sticky from dipping
chicken into honeyed batter. You can't decide
how serious this is.

Without lanterns
we cannot see the windmill spinning
its dark blue arms in the dark blue sky by the lake.

I do not hate you. It's just
that the weapons you keep to fight
death make me afraid.

I love you except when you are monkeying
your way across the bars
of philosophy, stressing we are masters of our fates.

Moving

I leave the couch where the plants swing
their shadows. Where I am going is
a painting in my mind. Sometimes you are
in it, sometimes not. In one picture
the bed is made, drapes billow. In another
the covers are a satin heap,
purple on the floor. The window frames
are packed with snow, the room painted
cold blues and greens that shine like ice.
I am going to another country
in the same room—this same room
in another city—clean, white,
separate from what changes
and from what's certain.
It is easier to go on foot
than to imagine being there.
When I get there,
my bags will be waiting. I have packed
in case I arrive.

Color at night

is simpler, harder
to identify. There are floods
of ocher. Purple seeps
inside, mountains flatten.

Who is this woman
begging for my body to
have its turn
as night does? She waits for hands

the color of stars
to reach for her, for the melon moon
to leak its streams of pearly
light into the sullen

green, deeper than the brown
holding its roots. She wants a man
who is a wolf with many tongues
who growls or is silent

and will swallow her
when he is finished—
that's what she wants:
to leave her lover

in the pale
raspberry glow
of an untimely rain
for a stranger touch.

The Rose Light

In a room
of objects
we could
endlessly
exchange things
and never be
satisfied.
But in your room,
with the rose glass
making the light
unreal and
the flat bed
set there
for no other
reason
than love,
the passing
of hands
over skin
lifts us still
further
into a realm
that makes
whatever we did
to get there
justifiable.

Back in the world
of giving
and taking

we are rats
sniffing
with vicious
hunger
for loopholes
in the golden rule.

Opals

Your face is framed
in the window of the familiar
coffee shop dense
with people in from the cold.

Opposite you
silence lingers. This is the end
of stages: the curtain closing
on long rehearsed and anticipated acts.

In this dingy city spot
our bodies glow—opals
of desire. Like tangled ribbons
words curl and fall—petals

from a bloom
where everything has already happened.
I'm angry that you're old
and I don't want death to be

what separates us. Let us peel
love from death's grip and see
the wound it has covered,
wisdomless and pleading.

Let the end be now. I watch
you leave, widening the dark
you are safe in. Teased by what
I remember, I think

the thoughts that loved me
as if they weren't mine.

Body of Water

Children's laughter leaves the beach at seven.
The sand is silent. Dragonflies, bulging with blood,
eyes popping, riding in tandem,
nip at the water. A path of bubbles appears.

You wait on dry land
with a towel, watching
my pink breasts float
on the blackening lake.

I am in a cold cellar breathing in
a violet color I have no memory of.

I look across that lake
and ask you about those strange gray shapes

hanging on the dark green trees.
You say it's just the last light

coming through. To me it seems like something
I could touch, something
I could tear off the branch
and take with me.

In My Silence

What's left of the past is not what was said
or remembered. It is here
in the way we open
to each other, as if we knew then
what we know now
but couldn't anticipate
what might come of it.

Didn't you know all this
was in my silence?
I knew
you didn't believe yourself,
I knew from the way you loved
I would remember
what you never told me.

A Myth Around Your Fingers

My brain, a cloud
around my thinking, and me, a myth
embodying an ancient world around your
fingers of fire and water moving
inside me, knowing
how to leave pleasure
on their tortuous course.
You lead the unhappy heart
inside my head
to a quiet long
yearned for. We arrive
at a haven as sure
as a cove molded
by its mountain. The earth
repeats its spin. Love
reverses its alchemy and
turns into its return.

Presence

You stopped over
in this country as if it
were a room enclosed by what was
always about to happen. The room retains
your presence. I keep seeing

startling shapes, almost water-like
waves of green. In the air
a tang like mint. Clouds gather
into a storm; shadows in different grays fall
crisscross. The plants, now interspersed with rain

clouds bend differently since you were last here.
They have reached some new understanding. I can tell
by the gentle curves in the cuttings, the bright rose
colors in the begonias demanding attention.
You came back to describe this all

differently:
that week
of rain, silver-
pink rivers
lying still

on a soft brown cloth,
streams of music making
a disappearing path
where, by a wooden house,
we swam in the dark.

The News

I can't let you stay
comfortable, flipping channels
while reclining in your chair,
watching golf carts

spin from hole to hole outside
the screened-in porch,
creating the same life
in the same room

we've come to know as tomorrow
again and again.
Even though the way
we've come to serve each other

beers and Cape Cod chips is sweet
and our bodies relax
at a toe rubbed
or a hand held, I've come

to hate the way
we ignore
the news
our unhappiness brings—

the intelligence
that could undo what
lets us
tolerate this.

Piston Force of Quiet

I.

I'm surprised you think I would never leave,
that I would sit like the trunk
of a tree, confirmed in my destiny,

weeping in the inner rings of time,
pest in a household
of carefully placed things.

II.

It's gone—the turn
of the stomach anticipating
all that will change,

the conviction
that our hearts did fly
in that light we made.

III.

You are alone with your cats. Your past
hangs on the walls, framed in metallic colors.
I love what is still in you,

when it speaks, suffers, slows down:
shy night that keeps going,
bottomless color that matches nothing.

IV.

Snow banks rise and swirl
outside the window, a bitter season traced
on the glass. We fold each feeling,

put them in neat piles—
white handkerchiefs warm from the iron.
It's time to release the piston

force of quiet.

Winds

The gray rain
disguises the day
then the disguise
is rained away.
The rain
is the day:
silver drops
on the pine needles.
Winds in your dream
came into my dream.

I couldn't let go
of your images, unearthly
storms that ushered in death,
mud deep around the tires,
the TV, loud with color
in the cloudy room,
a horse without a rider,
slick and wet, galloping.
My heart pounds, afraid
you won't find the storm
I'm in.

Definition

I keep turning
to the dictionary
to understand love. I pass
look, loud, lordly,
and *louse.*
Then I spot it, just a few lines down
from a picture of louver boards.
Love,
it tells me, is
"a feeling of strong personal attachment
induced by sympathetic understanding
or by ties of kinship;
ardent affection." It says
"See attachment."
I see attachment
defined as "strong liking
or even devotion as opposed
to affection, a feeling
more settled and regulated,
less intense than love,
which alone of the three
may connote passion."
I turn to *passion:*
"an enduring inflicted pain,
tortures or the like."
That is where love led me, once
I passed those sloping boards
set to shed rainwater,
the lantern-shaped cupolas
on the roofs of medieval buildings
designed to admit air
and provide for the escape of smoke.

71

Promise

You traverse existence as if
a universe you have proven

can be contained in your mind. Leaping
over lit moons, you label me

no longer shining. Once
a wished-upon star,

I stare now
like a nurse at death, her job over,

issues of right and care somehow
an old prison. Even sex, once

a mountain pass or a gust doubling over
all growth in its way,

now just floats us down
whitened smudges of sensation—scrawls

of light fade—then appear
to waken us to a spurned darkness

you want to explain
but it's as clear

as anything
you could say.

Airmail

While you're away I reconstitute
loss. This is my specialty—living
questions already answered. Outside

sundown fires the row
of hills where I glimpse
what I want. I want

a postcard of these hills
that says what this says:
missing, missing you,

till I hate
missing you.
I will be

happy and unhappy watching
the leaves shine
in their ordinary lives.

IV

I Want Your Chair

I Want Your Chair

There are a thousand ships in my bathtub.
I know this
because I am crazy. There is shampoo
in my hair and shit on the bottom
of my sandals—things I'd never think
of mentioning in our conversations.
Is this because you are not my friend
but my doctor? Your prescription reads:
"Utter only what concerns you."
I listen as I speak.
I listen as you speak.
I am always listening.
I can always hear you, here
in your presence or while sitting
in my tub with my thousand ships.
I send my ships around the world
to bring back voices. My friends are
voices I sit beside, body near, mind far.
To erase the distinction, I speak.
I must be a voice for them.
An immense curiosity
is erupting. I want to know the judge,
then dismiss him. And you, doctor,
I want your chair.
I want to ask you some questions
about yourself. How many hours do you sleep?
On what side of your body? Do you eat
immediately upon rising? Do you drink wine
with your dinner? Do you like large parties?
Would you rather
be a painter? Would you please
get out of my bathtub?

Emergency

I try to reach you at the fleabag hotel
in Chelsea. The drowsy clerk says,
"We only call residents to the phone
in an emergency. I can leave
a note in her box. Is it an
emergency?"

"Only if she's dead," I say.

I wait, the receiver at my ear,
picturing a phone on each floor
ringing in the carpeted corridors,
you in bed blending dark and light,
each day gray. The radio at night.
And when the timer snaps off the music
in the middle of a song,
you are watching the shadows shake
by candlelight.

The Taster's Choice stands half full
by a hot plate near your bed,
non-dairy creamer powders a chipped wooden chest,
the garbage is filled with tangerine peels
and Campbell's soup cans, punched in
with a ten-cent opener.

The receiver is cold and quiet
against my ear. I try to hear you
breathe.

A Wide Range of Pathology

They ask me:
"Why do you want to work here?"
Do you prefer working with psychotics
or neurotics? How has it come about
that you changed fields?
Do you still write poetry,
or was that just a passing interest?"

Mr. Head Doctor tries to interest me
in his program, puts his specs on his desk
and goes through the ins and outs
that make it diversified.
"You can go right into the homes of the families.
You can bring the family into the hospital.
We have long-term patients, short-term
patients, crisis intervention. We have
seminars, didactics, rounds, grand rounds.
We have SUPERVISION, one-way mirrors,
open wards, closed wards, half-price lunches
and excellent staff morale."

"And what do you have?" he asks
looking at the slight opening
between the second and third button
on my shirt that's a little
too tight.

"I have long-term experience, short-term
experience, intensive experience and testing
experience."

"Very good" he says.
"So why do you want to come here?"
"Because of the SUPERVISION.
I've heard wonderful things about it—
that it's both frequent and thorough.
Are you a SUPERvisor?"

"Yes, I am" he says.
"What's your orientation
may I ask?"
"I would say it totters
between common sense and Freud, but
I've been known to accommodate myself
to a student's needs."
"How sensible!"

"Anything else I can tell you?"
"Well, what kind of patient
do you generally get here?"
"We entertain a wide range of pathology.
A benefit of the program is a view
of the whole spectrum of mental disorders."
"That does sound like quite a spread."

Mr. Head Doctor returns
his specs to the bridge
of his nose, reaches,
indicating it's time for me to leave.
"I'm impressed," I say,
"with the range and depth
you seem to offer here at Mountain Head

80

Hospital. I do hope to hear from you."

        "Well, you show promise, Miss Pearl.
Up to now I would say you are one
of the more attractive candidates
I have seen. I would certainly like to hold
a slot open for you."

        "Thank you so much.
I'm sure I don't have to tell you
that Mountain Head is my very first choice."

Dream

Lying on the floor, purely pregnant,
fig round, just a stem of mood
visible, a foot.

I roll, embarrassed
at how low I place
myself. You look down

from your chair—
how high you seem from over here
where I am growing wide

and full of vowels.
My thoughts crackle like meteors,
loud in thin skin.

My fears, hoarded goods that fill
a sunken steamer trunk
seep into amniotic waters and spread

into a boundless moon
of blackness
till my flesh hurts.

If only I could take these babies
that won't stop growing inside
out. They flourish in my dark. Secrets

you listen for with your folded
hands. I know you're thinking
they will be born

alive and loving,
colored like honey and chocolate
and olives, with names

like Franz and Frieda. Even Lillian.
Then I'll stand up, stop, rest or
move again. At least there will be

a choice of what to use myself for.

Son and Father

He enjoyed subduing his emotions
by walking red setters on the frozen creek.

He remembered his father sorting
through mail before walking or feeding

the dogs. Pitying dogs
is a vivid feeling from his past.

He is still imprisoned in feeling
sorry for dogs. Whenever the mail comes,

he puts it aside and feeds his pups,
whether they're hungry or not.

When the creek isn't iced over,
he walks, calm as a lake, on

a road—a river
like a long window. He moves

at the same pace
as a bullet still in its gun.

Suicide

It distinguished you,
separated you from love
surrendered
in a way that let you call yourself
strong. This detail concluded
the conversation you were having
with yourself.

What made you dislodge yourself
from your bones
and become another bloody bruise
in the white morning sky, summoning
lawlessness
into the emptiness?.

Was it vengeance
or the truth of your life;
a twin
always the shadow
of someone real?

Blue Stones Set in Silver

She gravitates towards windows
while awake
while asleep.
The blond nurse holds her hand
dripping with blood
over the broken glass. Her fist
found its way
         through the clear pane
to the fresh air.
         And the rest of her
would have followed
but she froze
         not feeling the pain
         nor the fear
not answering to her name.
Her amber hair, like rope,
         moves
around her face,
         pocked
as with spilled red berries.
Black tears streak her hot flushed skin.
         She reaches for
the nurse's other hand and says,
"That's a beautiful ring.
I like the blue stones set in silver.
         I like the way
it looks on you."
         She pulls her hand away
from the nurse, from the bandage.
         "I like the way

the blood rolls over my skin
                  and onto the floor."
"Give me your hand," says the nurse.
She puts her hand
               in the hand with the glimmering ring
and lets her fingers be taped.
"Hold still now," says the nurse.
"But it doesn't hurt,"
               she says, keeping still.
"It only looks that way to you."

This Spanish Cloth

After all these years of marriage,
I don't know how to be single. I need
a new mind. Do you know what it's like
to feed yourself thoughts that end

love and then go on and on
to betray you? I'm well on my way
to becoming a bag lady. What can you do
with 6 credits towards a B.A.? Thrive on

rescue fantasies? I like this guy
Theodore, but there's this fucking
gorgeous rocket scientist,
Greek, tall, funky downtownish. He talks

about wave physics and CO_2 levels;
the other is writing
about a freak storm.
and looks like a wolf—

silvery eyes, beard, deep voice.
The physicist has a girlfriend
in Canada. She's coming
in. I'm sewing a pocket

into this old leather coat. I love
this Spanish cloth. It's more than
I need. I keep everything
in big, deep, beautiful pockets

so I don't have to carry a bag.
I have a lot of treasures
no one sees. Do you have scissors?
Sometimes I think you must think

I'm weird. I feel bad
for you, that you might hate me
and not be able to say it.

Billy

I'm not a good person.
Could you stop
hollering at me?
When I say hollering it means
you don't want me
to do something.

Silence is hollering.
Stop it.
My favorite Beatles song is
Across the Universe.
I'm usually mad. Whenever I'm not mad,
I'm not happy.

When the Beatles lost their mad feelings,
they didn't have any other feelings.
Whenever I'm not mad, it means
I don't have feelings, I have problems.
I have more problems than anyone
in my family.

Sometimes I feel sad,
never happy. Actually,
I have three feelings,
mad, sad and scared....

Working on a Collage at Bellevue

Her eyes are pasty blue
like a burnt-out bulb.
She calls herself
          "The Fat Ballerina."
Asks me
        if I ever saw her swans.
Paints
        a red swan on the blue horizon;
waits for it to dry
        and drops in
a black eye.
         A red moon rises
in her mind
        and appears behind a tree.

Mamma Leaves

"I'm not a Virgin, mamma,
and when I don't come home on time
I'm doing everything
you are afraid I'm doing
because you are afraid I'm doing it
and cause I'm afraid too, Mamma,
that I'm everything you're afraid I am."

With a hint of auburn bleached
into her black bangs, she attracts
guys who play the killing music
in the school yard and laughs with them
a laugh that sparkles like a six-year-old
who thinks she'll always be the same.
They have her listen in shadows
to how they survived their spare
lives in the cold stench of cells.
As their blood-eyed passion hooks
her loneliness, their pierced nose
hoops are the only gleam
she remembers from the sweaty air
and the tight knots of beer
still going down like a blur
you can't push away.

Mamma knows unhappiness isn't safe,
so gives her chores. She scrubs rusty
metal cans, polishes splintering wood,
licks green stamps, prays she could go
crazy enough to avoid her fate.

Mamma gives her a cross on a gold chain
and packs a suitcase. They enter the ward.
Mamma is kerchiefed, her wire rollers bulging
from the back of her head. The suitcase
is put down. She watches
mamma leave. The door
unlocks and locks again.

Science Experiment

A lamp is reflected in the window
in a way that makes it look like
a planet in the sky.
Sometimes I see myself in you

in a way that I mistake
for myself. Other times I see myself
in a way that is just
a mistake. I place you

in the path of light
in different ways, changing
how the body moves on glass—
first clear in its outline, but gutted out,

then blurred in detail,
finally photo-like,
as you go on
and out into a night

that has its own life
but obligingly carries
our fragile luminosity through
endless dimensions.

All I really had and lost
of you is how I saw you.
Who is to be blamed
for that?

Without a Trace

"Birds kept singing
throughout Buenos Aires
though universities froze
careers and made education a form
of torture. Professors left the country,

sent their children to neighbors.
If you believed in anything
other than what you were told
they made you disappear.

There was great temptation
to learn to believe lies,
to learn not to feel the pain of forgetting
the way back. It started when my lover

was pushed from a plane
because he sympathized with the workers.
I went into a mental hospital
when I was 20—35 years ago—

all bruise, soul split, bare
arms under a tangle of hair.
They said it was my genes
and they could do nothing

about it, that mother was
schizophrenic as well,
though she lived to 88
married three times."

"And in your country,"
she asked, "was there such murder?"
"No. They murdered our capacity to know
that the dark was a substance

that could have nourished us
had we known we were hungry.
The years of searching
led only to searching

till the desire to change
reminded us of the decay beyond
each turn. The Sixties did away with bodies
whose souls threatened the existing world

and murdered souls whose bodies were needed
to keep the world existing.
They packaged dreams
and when we did not leap for them,

our hatred was called just
our need for hatred. No,
there was no need
to gather us in stillborn dawns,

and prod us with high-voltage shocks.
We had learned to disbelieve
in eternity, were perfected
to reproduce their dreams

and not know ours were missing."

V

Free

As He Drives

*"I do a lot of washing. I wash everything.
If I could only get this clean once, before I die."*
      — Margaret Atwood

The pencil is stuck in the book at a place
where Buddy never rescues his sister
from her whirlwind dreams of a Kodachrome home
as she licks green stamps in poor light,

and where he never saves her from cleaning
the Buick with paper towels
that lick the dust, revealing
color like wet light

reflecting a world of roofs and stars.
Buddy never regrets the ease
with which he drives away,
ending his desire

to rescue his sister. Her catlike hair,
deep sunflower eyes and loose stained teeth
always shocked him into thinking,
"Too many regrets, decay, not in her right mind."

Her hand never had a reason to turn
the TV, or stove, or radio off or on,
but it did anyway because it was no different
from his own hand

moved by thoughts taking him
where he didn't want to go.

He listened to her, as if through
a dollhouse window, tell him

his bandana smelled of clean, white
summer. Now wind fragrant as cornbread
turns sleep to morning coffee.
Her heart was his room

cold as the lies he left her
breathing in. Her innocence
loses beauty as he drives.

Moving. I Stand

At the Artist's Colony I'm given a shelf
and half a refrigerator, two keys, a towel,
a top and bottom sheet. My desk,

an unfinished board on two trestles,
overlooks a gray road. A map
of Ulster County, New York, hangs low

on the wall. I'm the new person:
a first name in their
minds, flat as a face on a coin.

My husband and children are backing
out of the dark driveway. A thinning string
of feeling holds us. But,

my son says,"Let's get the family away
from these hippies. You fit, mom, not us."
The gold van pulls away.

The stars, as if coughed out
of my children's throats,
enter my room ahead of me.

They wait
for me to come in
with the key.

Apple Core

His paintings lush with light
show covert processes
changing the shape of the forest
to dry land exhibited
in water, and a once red

apple to its remains.
He warns me not to look
at any one of them for more
than ten minutes. That's enough
to see the picture hidden

in the picture. "If you gaze longer
it will become your own
and you will lose
the feeling it is intended
to create in you."

What was left
of devouring—
brown, disposable—
is captured like the time of
day in a four-by-six space.

Mousetrap

All these stale cakes, crumbling
and hardening, I hoard
because they are free. Like a sorceress

foreseeing drought and famine
over long nights,
I dress these tarts and crumb cakes

in soft, white napkins, pile them
into Grand Union sacks and set them
in closets safe from moonlight.

Even hunger wouldn't tempt me
now...silver-haired mice
scratch in the walls.

They wait for dark to feast
on the piles of crumbs
on which they hope

to flourish. My waste creates their desire.
I plot to catch them
in glue or spring traps, imagine them

losing their struggle with the taste of flour
still in their mouths.
My envy is their doom.

Correspondence Between Two Poets

I wish I knew what I meant when I sent
that letter and what is meant by

sending a letter. I wrote to someone
old whom I never saw

except when I was young. I said things
I wished I'd said when I was young

and did not want to say now.
So you would never know

what I wanted to say then, I said
what I thought in the moment. You'll read

the words as if you remember me, but never
met me. You think that since I am

a poet, when I skydive into
self-deception I know it,

and even at the bottom could
rise again on words.

You will think I call silence *meteor*
or *scaffold* or *stone*, brighten up

nowhere, tend
the sunlight in the theoryless

recesses of the ocean and sometimes destroy
parts of the past—oracles, antiques,

crusaders—with whatever is at hand,
just to make room for an image

that never was.

Lost at Loehmann's

You said: "If I'm not here,
it means
I'm shopping."
"Is that what *it* means?"
I ask,
"if *you* are not here?"

Free

In a bed of soft, dead, orange-
brown leaves lay two rusting black
muffin tins, with a sign reading, Free.

The lady in the Hopper house behind the scraggly
lawn imagines cupcakes that will rise again
in the old black tins. Whoever takes them

could use those thin pastel papers—
no danger then of harm
from the rust. She gathers loose tiles,

a dented watering can, a dusty
lace doily and the plastic
plant on top of it, each

in their turn to replace
the tins, the one for 12 miniature muffins,
the other for 4 jumbo ones,

when they are taken from the nest
of fall colors, on the corner
of McCuin and Main Street.

That word *Free* makes some turn back,
their stride interrupted like a long story
they were being offered a say in.

In the Middle of Dinner

We come unexpectedly early—in the middle of dinner with
their other guests. The children—ours sticky and wild from
traveling, theirs just bathed, scented and robed—are taken
to the backyard to blow bubbles and catch fireflies.

After unpacking the car, we are offered what's left of their
meal. My uncle, the reason we came, accepts hugs. His
eyes speak, diamond-bright in their darkening shadows.
Pounds have been eaten away by cancer. His skin, a thin
tissue, is about to dissolve and let him out.

I eat meat on skewers
and plump cooked vegetables
leaking juices all over my plate,
accept a beer, join a conversation
about whether secrets in the night
are silent company or cure illness

when they come out like bare
feet walking—quiet on the hot
stones of fear. My uncle coughs, tries to hide
his face, eyes, tears
so death will look like
only a thought

within him, not a contagious mood
that's spread to all our cells.
The children want their pie.
Hands are raised
for ice cream, the dishes cleared,
dessert forks placed on folded napkins.

I ask who wants Lemon Mist—
Red Zinger—Sleepy Time?

The Job of Pain

When I mistake warm silence for the hollow
in the boat, or mind for an ocean,

or a strategy for bringing cargo
from mass graves into the imagined

as the boat itself, consequences emerge—
I need to be ahead of, awaiting them

as if I were infected, all along,
with the ink of

not yet printed news—the darkness of
trying to say what I knew

would happen and hoped to avoid.
If I choose not to choose

to take on what is passed down—
a hill of shoes and a town in ruins,

like black paper homes standing
silhouetted in silver air

beneath a pink sky—
I am certain

death will not end
what has not changed.

0 0 0

"...and the nothing that is."
— *Wallace Stevens*

We hear dreams, see their path,
like snakes' approach. They are
cleverer than attention
to their ways, stronger than resolve

to survive them. They lift us high
unafraid of a planet
that cannot explain things
as well as they do. We lean back

as we move through the zeroes. A light
beams in the darkening at the end
of this century, evidence of miracles
locked away. The zeroes are stationary

portholes rimmed with silver
holding out an ocean, a sampling of black
that means black, but is circled
as if it is the wrong answer.

We watch for those taking shape
from crematorium ash, who have been
resting while we lived haunted
by lives cut in half, nines that vowed

never to be nothing, now nothing.
Enlightenment, itself a morning
gone by. Now there is
only confusion. It is safe. No truth

has awakened sleep yet.
No certainty enters
our heads. This summer night
is all darkness

and the Atlantic Ocean barely a whisper
in one little girl's life.

I Want Your Chair
CD Listing

Photo credit: Stanley Marcus

Elaine Schwager is a poet, practicing psychoanalyst, psychotherapist, teacher and screenwriter, living in New York City with her husband and two children. She has had poems in *Rattapallax, Literal Latté, Writ* (Toronto), *The World* (St. Mark's Poetry Project), *Minding the Gap, Drunken Boat, Armadillo, Promethean,* among other publications. Her poems have also been in two anthologies: *It Is the Poem Singing in Your Eyes* (Harper and Row) and *City in All Directions* (Macmillan). She has been awarded residencies at The MacDowell Colony, The Woodstock Guild and The Vermont Studio Center.